Pam at Bat

by Jessica Quilty
illustrated by Nicole Wong

Target Skill Consonants *Dd/d/* and *Kk/k/*
High-Frequency Words *see, look*

Scott Foresman
is an imprint of

PEARSON

Little Pam can see Kim bat.

Look! Kim can bat!

Did Pam see Kim bat?

Little Pam can see Dan bat.

Look! Dan can bat!

Did Pam see Dan bat?

Look! Tim can bat.
Did Pam see Tim bat?

Look! Pam can bat.
Bat, Pam, bat!

Look! Pam ran!

Pam ran and ran!